DOMESTIC

One man's story of living in abuse and how to get out

by

H.S. Daniels

Copyright ©2021 by H.S. Daniels (Higher Ground Books & Media)
All rights reserved. No part of this publication may be reproduced in any form, stored in a retrieval system, or transmitted in any form, or by any means (electronic, mechanical, photocopying, recording or otherwise) without prior permission by the copyright owner and the publisher of this book.

Scripture taken from the HOLY BIBLE, NEW INTERNATIONAL VERSION®. NIV®. Copyright © 1973, 1978, 1984 by International Bible Society. Used by permission of Zondervan. All rights reserved worldwide.

Higher Ground Books & Media
Springfield, Ohio.
http://highergroundbooksandmedia.com

Printed in the United States of America 2021

Domestic

About this Book

I want to start by saying that my intention with this book is not to speak poorly of my ex-wife, to excuse my own behavior in the relationship, or to find my claim to fame. Although there are many aspects of my story that would have made for a more dramatic read,
I chose not to include them because they would not be helpful to the reader. I included events that make good examples, to better help those who may find themselves in a similar situation.

My hope is that men and women alike will see the warning signs of a manipulative and abusive partner and learn to get away before they are in a relationship with that person, those that are in an abusive relationship will learn how to safely get out of it, and those that are out will learn to heal and find a healthy relationship the right way.

I recognize my position to treat the mother of my children with respect and thus have taken all reasonable precautions to protect her image and identity: the names of individuals (including myself) have been changed, the names of towns and locations have been changed, and some dates may have been changed to protect those involved in this story.

Although some details may have been changed, the events themselves are real; this is not a work of fiction.

Introduction

You may have heard the old adage "there's plenty of fish in the sea", but equally important, and frankly under-expressed, is that the areas in which you fish and the type of bait you use are going to determine what type of fish you catch. Not to mention the season we choose to begin our outing.

Allow this to be the first, and possibly most important piece of advice you take from this book. Are you coming fresh off of a break-up, going to the bar, or dating app for a quick replacement? That's something that most of us have done; looked to immediately fill the void left by a bad relationship. We begin fishing without knowing what we are looking for, or even who we really are as a person. We just need to catch a fish, and quickly, regardless of what type of fish it is. We blindly hook fish and hope they are the perfect one.

I urge you to look at HOW your relationship started. The beginning of a relationship is the foundation of what you build together. Though we may not have ever predicted the terrible things that would happen to us, and sometimes there simply were no warning signs, but quite often there are signs that could have helped us avoid a terrible experience if we just stopped and looked.

This book will consist of three essential parts: First, I will tell my story and my experience with domestic violence, control, addiction, and manipulation in my marriage. Second, we will look at the flags, warning signs, and what action could be taken to safely get out of an abusive relationship. Third, we will discuss how to heal and have a healthy relationship after having come from an abusive past.

I feel this book is for everyone, even if you find yourself in the middle of a happy and perfect marriage - awareness is so vital so that it can be shared with those who may experience an abusive relationship.

Thank you for reading, please take the time to review this book after you are finished, and share it with friends and family.

Part One

Damage

Domestic

Chapter 1
The Mask is Gone

65...70...75...80, I watched my speedometer climb steadily as I accelerated my car down the hill. The highway had been clear up to this point, so the semi in the oncoming lane was my only chance. I rolled down my window to feel the wind on my face and gripped the steering wheel tightly, this was it—with any luck, they would even rule it an accident instead of a suicide. My eyes glossed over with tears.

I felt my phone vibrate. I had almost forgotten what it felt like to get a text, I hadn't gotten one in days. I looked at the message, from my old partner from work, "Hey, just wanted to check on you. I miss you. This sucks."

It might not seem like much, but that single message was enough to keep me in my own lane. I took my foot off of the gas until the needle fell back to 65, then continued on for another 15 miles. I had a few hundred dollars, enough for some time in a hotel. I had been sleeping in my car, but I needed rest and to clean up before court in the morning.

I looked at my hands, squeezing the steering wheel and turning my knuckles white. The hands of a real criminal now, I supposed. Only a week prior, my life was what most people would call perfect—how did it get to this?

All of the years spent hiding behind a mask had worn the mask down, and now the truth was out. The happy little family everyone saw would be exposed as liars, cheaters, abusers, and addicts. The mask was gone, and I felt frightened and alone.

Chapter 2
Building Starts with the Foundation

Let me set the scene: I had just turned 20 and had been very fortunate in my career. I worked at a retail store since I was 17 and was quickly promoted over the years. For a 20-year-old, I made good money, drove a nice car, and went on a lot of dates. I wouldn't describe myself as rich, but describing my demeanor as "the playboy lifestyle" wouldn't be too far off. My weekends were usually spent drinking and partying, while looking for someone to take home at the end of the night.

I had dated yet another girl who accompanied me to many alcohol-fueled parties until the relationship ended when she wound up cheating on me at one of those parties. As the relationship ended, I hooked up with another party girl—Carmen. She was different from most of the people I had dated, or even befriended, mostly because she had moved here from another state. I grew up in a small town in Montana, she was from New York. She moved to Montana with her now ex-husband for his work, they got divorced, she got a job at my store, and she showed up to a lot of the parties. Now we were in bed together before her divorce was even finalized, and she would soon be my next girlfriend... or so I thought.

After a very short drunken, sexual relationship, Carmen was pregnant. If I had included a proper introduction of myself, I would have mentioned that I already had a daughter with my highschool sweetheart. Although we now got along great and made the best out of our baby daddy/baby momma relationship, we initially struggled to make it work. The birth of our child started with brutal court proceedings and slamming each other in hopes of winning custody. The thought of going through that again with Carmen was terrifying. I couldn't do it.

I told myself that I needed to try to make the relationship work for the baby's sake. Around this time, her lease was up in her apartment so I asked her to move in with me, and our life together began.

***

Fast forward a couple of years and things are only moving up in my life; I got hired on with the city police department, thus ending my seemingly endless retail career. The PD job was great, it was a job I was truly proud of, the pay and benefits were good, the one downside was the rotating schedule. We would rotate day shift and night shift every 4 months, I knew from my retail days that I was not a good night shift person, but I toughed it out. Carmen would stay home with our toddler and newborn baby while I worked (we had another baby about a year and a half after the first was born).

I sat out on the lawn cooking burgers on the grill and watching the kids sit in the grass, and thought to myself "this is the life people want, isn't it?". The unfortunate truth for me and many other relationships is that the glossy surface of the relationship barely covers the brittle structure crumbling away beneath.

Discussion

Looking back, I can now see as clear as day how our relationship was wrong from the very start. Where do I begin? I was jumping from relationship to relationship, which was teaching me to use women as a sort of emotional Band-Aid, and once one started to peel off I needed to stick a fresh one on.

I didn't love myself. Having a relationship meant I didn't have to be alone with myself; my faults and failures, my innermost demons.

A relationship that is quickly sexual is not one built on respect. I didn't respect her from the first moments, if I respected her - I wouldn't have used her.

Even though I wouldn't have said at the time I was looking for marriage, or even a serious relationship—it should have been clear that we were not set up to have one. "The divorce is pending" is no justification to start a new relationship, I slept with a married woman and she cheated on her husband. I've heard of situations (in fact it happened to me) where the divorce drug on for YEARS because of legal issues or other unusual circumstances that tied things up in the court process. I can understand in that scenario beginning to look for someone to date, but certainly being open with them about the situation.

This was not that however, there were no unusual circumstances—they were pending divorce, and it went rather quickly from what I recall. Perhaps she was using me as a bandaid just as I was using her.

If you aren't healed and healthy after a breakup, you only bring the bad stuff with you to your next relationship. Your past follows you forever until you become truly free from it.

How can you apply this to your life? If you are starting a new relationship, look at how that relationship began. What was your foundation? What are you hoping to get out of the relationship, and what steps are you taking to reach that goal?

If you are single, keep these things in mind. You shouldn't be worried so much about hunting for your next relationship, but rather preparing yourself to be healed and ready to be in that relationship. What steps are you taking to set a good foundation despite the past baggage or damage that has been done? You can build on top of the bad foundation.

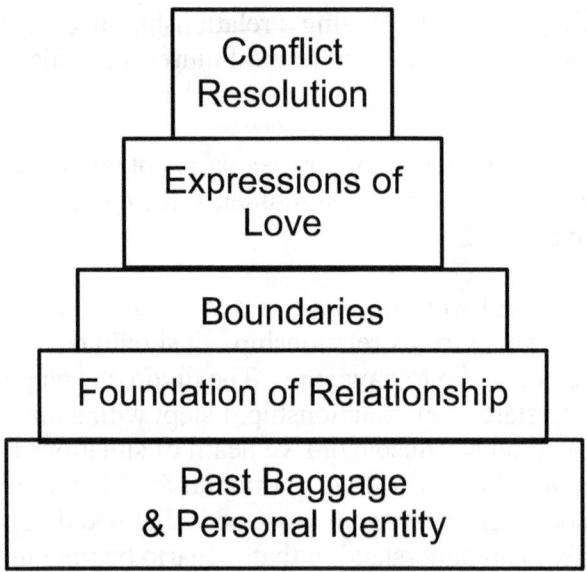

Past Baggage and Personal Identity refer to your past experiences and upbringing. How you view yourself plays a crucial role in how you treat others. How you were treated in the past makes a significant impact on how you view a relationship is supposed to be.

Foundation of Relationship means how and when the relationship started, this usually is determined by what we view as "normal" based on our experiences and upbringing. Starting a new relationship to cover up the pain of a break-up is a negative start to build a foundation on. A "drunken mistake" is not a positive foundation either. The *how* and *when* a relationship started are important to its future success.

Boundaries are the lines you set in a relationship, what you will tolerate and what you will simply not put up with. These boundaries are set from how the relationship began. If you don't want to be married to a drunk, but you met your boyfriend in a bar—there might be a problem with the foundation. If you don't want to be cheated on, but you started dating when they cheated *with* you, then there is probably a problem with the foundation.

Expressions of Love are the ways that affection is shown; hand-holding, kissing, compliments, date nights, etc. Expressions of love stem directly from boundaries, because that is how your significant other views a healthy relationship to be. A highly sexual relationship that offers no other signs of affection stem from unhealthy boundaries. "He only wants sex but never takes me on dates," is the result of the initial boundaries being set wrong. The relationship likely started highly sexual, this was allowed in the beginning, it was built into the foundation, and now the signs of affection reflect how it all began.

Conflict Resolution means how problems are solved in the relationship. If they are solved with yelling, hitting, getting drunk, or cheating, then there is a problem in the signs of affection which ultimately stems from the foundation of the relationship. Conflict should never be solved by yelling, insults, or violence. We will look at this more in the next chapter.

The takeaway from this discussion, is to look at the foundation of your relationship. It is not too late to re-lay that foundation and make it right.

Chapter 3
Resolving Conflict

A typical day for me went something like this: I would wake up early (when I was on day shift), cook breakfast because I love cooking, go to work, come home, cook dinner, bathe the kids, put them to bed and read them a story, go to bed myself (maybe after a little TV), and repeat. When I got home from work, Carmen would want to go out to the bar with her friends. She would say that she had been with the kids all day while I was at work and needed a break.

The first vivid memory I have of a real, major frustration with Carmen was when the baby would cry at night. Our oldest was a sick little fella and had a rough time sleeping and transitioning into a crib. I am not a believer that the woman should be responsible for getting up with a baby, raising a child is a team effort. But for sake of practicality, when the baby is crying at 3 am and I have to get up at 5 am for work (not to mention, I have a job that I must be rested and vigilant for), and Carmen didn't work at all, she should have been more willing to let me sleep. Yet night after night, I found myself up with Marcus (our son) over and over so Carmen could rest. It never killed me to get up with him, but it was the first time I felt alone in our relationship, and I'll never forget that feeling.

Time wore on and Marcus could finally sleep through the night, and now it was Stephen's turn (our youngest) to cry and transition into a crib. The same routine of me getting up all night long ensued, and once again I survived having to get up every night by myself.

One particular evening, I was working the night shift at the PD and was involved in a traffic accident call. After administering first aid, I went home to change uniforms from the blood-covered one I was wearing. It was approximately 1:00 am when I got home and found Carmen outside on the porch talking to a friend of hers. I said hello, only thinking it moderately strange to see her up so late. When I went inside, there was Stephen, crying his eyes out over a pile of vomit. He had gotten sick in the night, threw up, and couldn't find his mom to help him. I was so frustrated, but we agreed this was a simple misunderstanding and moved on from it as no big deal.

A month later, I returned home in the middle of the night again to change clothes as mine were covered in OC spray. This time, I found my mother sleeping on the couch and Carmen nowhere to be found. My mother woke up when I came inside.

"Mom?" I asked, "Where's Carmen?"

"She asked me if I could come and babysit for a bit. She wanted to go to dinner with some friends."

The blank stares we exchanged were enough of an explanation. Carmen went to dinner with friends, didn't come home and my mother had fallen asleep waiting for her. It was almost midnight now. I panicked, wondering if she was hurt or in need of help.

I called her phone and she answered amongst the unmistakable background noise of a bar. She was nearly incoherent, and a friend of hers took the phone away and chatted with me.

The friend apologized, not knowing we didn't know where they were and brought Carmen home. She was too drunk to have a discussion with, I had to take the rest of the night off because I couldn't leave the children home with Carmen passed out. It certainly wasn't my mother's responsibility to stay though she offered, because she's kind like that.

The next day, after sobering up, Carmen and I were able to talk about what happened. I wasn't the sweet and gentle husband I had been all this time, I was tired of being the only parent to our kids so she could run around and party - it was time for her to grow up. We stood in the hallway arguing; me yelling at her to grow up, and her yelling at me to quit being a jerk. I cannot remember the exact sentence that did it, but it was something along the lines of me telling her that I had three kids at home instead of two when *wham*, she smacked me in the face.

My reaction was not calm or dignified like I would have hoped, I used the momentum of the slap to push her away, causing her to fall onto the floor and cry. I walked away, went outside, and sat in my car. I looked at myself in the mirror and wondered what to do next.

She called my phone as I sat outside, and we continued to argue. I told her I think she needed to find somewhere else to stay for a while because I didn't want her in the house.

She paused before replying, "then I'm going to call the cops and tell them you threw me down."

I hung up the phone, looked at myself in the mirror again, a small spot of broken skin was on my lip where she had hit me. I thought about how that call to the police would go—not in her favor. Although the fear of that call consumed me, that could cost me my career, my reputation, leverage in a divorce, I could lose the kids. I became so afraid of that call, so I returned inside and did my best to make up with her.

It was a bad day. She was tired, hungover, depressed, I was frustrated and angry. This wasn't "us" we told each other and decided to leave it in the past.

Discussion

Obvious red flags, right?

First off, let me say that raising a baby is hard and exhausting. It's exhausting with two parents! It's not a job meant for one person, it's meant to be a team effort. When you find yourself in those moments of exhaustion, but can still look at your spouse and want to help them and be there for them, that's what makes those moments bearable.

I don't fault people who struggle with alcohol, I had no problem with quitting drinking after becoming a dad, but others struggle and I understand that. If you or your partner is unable to take care of the children because of drinking, please seek help. There are many support groups that can provide assistance to you.

Another element here, though somewhat hidden is deception: Carmen didn't blatantly lie to me but was certainly lying through means of omission. I didn't know where she was, I didn't know she was drinking. I didn't know these things because she hid them. If you hide things from your spouse, it's a lie. If your significant other is hiding things from you, ask yourself WHY they feel the need to hide that from you. Because they're embarrassed? Because they are afraid of you? In hindsight, I could have been more supportive during this time and tried to provide help rather than criticism.

Lastly, and the most obvious of course is a fight turning physical. This is indicative that highly emotional situations will be handled aggressively. Disagreements are normal in a relationship, but disrespect is not and should never be! This was the first time that things ever got so heated or got physical, but it was also the most serious argument we had to that point. It's easy to pass it off saying we were upset or drunk, but the fact of the matter is tough times will come, time and time again. When those tough times come, you need a partner fighting with you, not against you.

If you take nothing from this chapter, please take this: if they hit you once, they will do it again. The tools you use for conflict go to the top of the toolbox to use the next time.

```
┌─────────────────────────────────────────┐
│         Conflict Resolution Toolbox     │
├─────────────────────────────────────────┤
│                                         │
│   Violence                              │
│                                         │
│                        Abuse            │
│              Lies                       │
│                                         │
│       _____          │
│                                         │
│                 Truth                   │
│                                         │
│                        Empathy          │
│   Healthy                               │
│                                         │
│              Values                     │
│                                         │
└─────────────────────────────────────────┘
```

Humans, by nature, learn by trial-and-error. If something works once, we will use that same tool or strategy again and again. If someone uses violence, lying, abuse, or threats to solve conflict, it goes to the top of their toolbox to use the next time.

If a heated argument leads to insults and pushing, the next argument will lead to those places much quicker. Be aware of phrases like "it will never happen again", because chances are, it will. It will happen again unless something is done to correct the problem, or you get out of the relationship.

Make sure to put healthy discussion, truth, and empathy at the top of YOUR toolbox so they are not buried by unhealthy conflict resolution strategies.

Chapter 4
Being Controlled

With that out of the way, it seemed as if things would once again be fine, the kids were older and going to preschool now. Carmen wanted a job to keep her occupied during the day and applied to a few places, finally receiving an offer as a housekeeper for a hotel chain. It was perfect for our scenario, she worked in the mornings and could be off in time to pick up the kids if I were running late or working the night shift.

I came home one day for her to tell me that they had let her go, I never asked why—it didn't really matter, she was upset and 'these things happen'. I consoled her, and about a month later she had a different job.

One of the more prominent things I recall from this time period is a friendship with one of Carmen's friends, named Erica. Erica came by quite often, the two were virtually inseparable, and it was relieving because I got along great with Erica. She was funny and overall quite pleasant. It didn't last, eventually, Erica stopped coming by and moved away for a job or college.

There was a day when Erica's car broke down, Carmen was at work, so I went and gave her a ride. We chatted, laughed, and I dropped her off, that was it. I told Carmen some of the jokes that were told, and that was the last time I saw Erica. I know now, years later, that Erica stopped coming by because Carmen told her I didn't want her around and didn't like her. How bizarre, right?

A few months later, Carmen needed a minor medical procedure done in a town a few hours away (remember I'm from a small town, so it's normal to travel to a hospital). She brought her female friend with her for company and got a hotel room for the night. She returned the next day and let me know that the procedure went well.

***
So here we are, a few days later, sitting on the couch watching a movie as I played a mindless game on my phone.

"What are you doing?" she asks

"Playing a game."

"Let me see."

We stare at each other for a moment. I turn the phone toward her so she can see what I'm doing. Confused, almost shocked by the request, but wanting to alleviate whatever had her concerned.

This continued and escalated intensely. To the point where I caught her going through my phone while I was sleeping.

On some occasions, like when I was late coming home from work, she would insist on performing oral sex on me so that she could taste and see if I had been cheating. I understand this is a bit vulgar, and I apologize; but acts such as these are private--even embarrassing. It's not something that someone would feel comfortable discussing with others, which is important because it kept me controlled by her—I didn't feel as if I could talk to anyone about it.

About a month later, I had a conversation at work with my supervisor. Carmen has confronted a female colleague of mine and told her not to talk to me. I was so embarrassed, I almost quit the police department. On some level, I had learned to accept that Carmen was overtly jealous, and overreacted. She always told me it was because she loved me so much and was just afraid of losing me.

More often than not though, Carmen's jealous outbursts didn't make me feel loved, they made me feel embarrassed. Making a scene in public, or to my friends or coworkers was not sweet or romantic—it was the opposite, it was controlling. Now she had embarrassed me in front of my coworkers by being jealous of a female colleague who had done nothing wrong. Everyone at work would see my controlling, jealous wife. Everyone would know they shouldn't invite me anywhere, talk to me, or be my friend, or they might cause a scene.

At this point, I will admit, I was completely emotionally

detached from the relationship. The accusations and suspicion were stressful enough, but now causing a scene with my place of employment—it was too much.

We had another one of the many serious conversations we've had up to this point, which ended with her crying. I was calm and respectful, but clear when I explained that I believed we should get a divorce. I was miserable.

Despite her tears, I was adamant and left the room before she became too emotional. She could see that there was no winning me over, not anymore.

But she found a way that she hadn't tried before and took a razor to her wrist. She told me that she couldn't live without me, I was her everything, she loved me and the kids and didn't want that to fall apart.

This was not the first time she had threatened suicide, and it wouldn't be the last. My concerns were of the kids, not of her. She would never let me take them without a fight, I couldn't stay with her while we had a custody battle, but I was worried about their safety if I left them alone with her. I reluctantly agreed to not file for divorce yet.

I tried to determine what to do next and went to work time after time again, numb like a zombie, while coworkers gave me uncomfortable glances.

Discussion

Write this down, "I am not property". Seriously, write it down and remind yourself of it every single day. Your partner has no business telling you who you can and cannot talk to, or telling someone they cannot talk to you. They don't own you. Hopefully, if there is a concern, it can be handled in a way that is respectful to both parties. I never understood the whole tough attitude "you talking to my girlfriend?". It's not romantic, it's controlling. You aren't their property.

The story at the beginning of the chapter, about Erica, was a situation of manipulation. Carmen didn't like me making friends with Erica. So, she told Erica that I didn't like her or want her around to keep her away from me. I'm not sure if she was worried we'd have an affair, or if she was jealous, but that doesn't matter— Carmen viewed me as hers, I was her property, and she wouldn't let another woman ruin that. To what extent would it go? Carmen already showed that she would confront a coworker, embarrass me. Would she start a fight? She would expect me to be flattered by her passion, rather than humiliated.

Now the trust thing, it's a strange situation honestly. Today, in my new life and a new marriage, my wife and I don't feel the need to go through each other's phones or anything else. It's disrespectful. If I ever did ask, I have no doubts she would show me and vise versa, but why would I ever ask?. We had to earn our way to this point of course. Let me say this: if you have a concern about your partner, ask them. If you can't believe their answer, then you need to question being in the relationship in the first place.

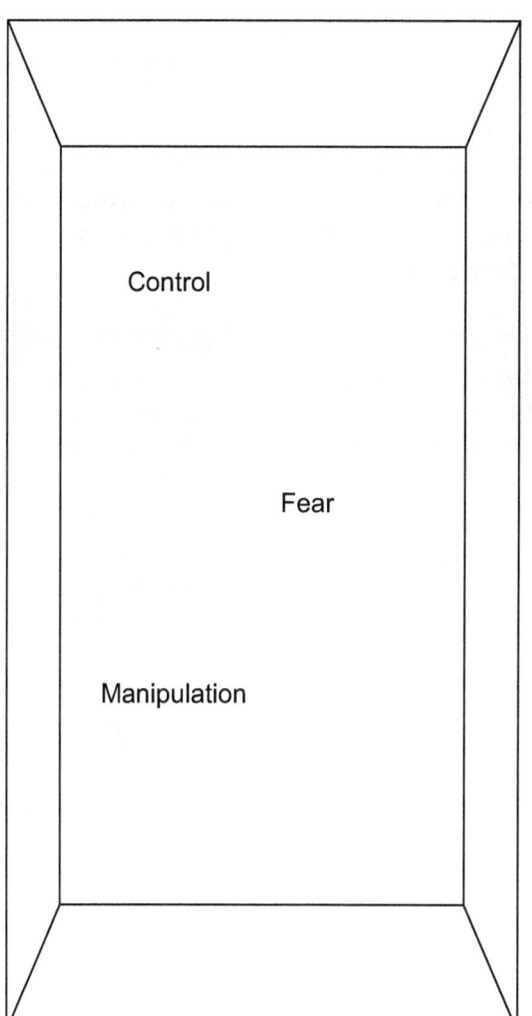

The illustration above depicts a box or a room. The room is used as a method to control the relationship through means of fear, manipulation, or physical control. Whereas outside of the box lies respect, trust, and teamwork.

You cannot have trust if you are living under control. As long as someone is controlling you, they will never trust you. You cannot have respect or teamwork so long as you are living in fear and manipulation under their control.

The relationship will be doomed to fail because the more you grasp for freedom, respect, trust, teamwork, equality, or just being treated humanely, the more they will tighten the confines of the box to attempt to retain control of the relationship. It is and will always be a one-sided relationship.

Chapter 5
Control and Sabotage

It may seem as if I have been an innocent victim thus far, I assure you that I was not. I hold some responsibility for the failures of the relationship and was far from innocent during its downfall. My job was to be a leader and protector, I did not do that job.

I was visiting with a friend, he stopped by but lived in another town—the one where Carmen went for her procedure. He was asking how she was doing and such, and asked who the guy was that was with them.

I pondered for a moment. I knew she went with a female friend...and she has a boyfriend, so it must have been her friend's boyfriend.

"No, I saw him," he replied, "the other guy. There were two."

I'm not sure if it's an actual cliche or I just made it up, but all the while she was suspicious of me cheating was because she was cheating. I should have suspected that more, I'm not sure why it didn't occur to me before. The cheater always suspects they are being cheated on.

This was around the time that I began to cheat on my wife. It wasn't a one-person affair, it was just small hookups much like those from my younger days.

Suddenly, I got hit with some good fortune. A nearby city police department had an opening, it was a dream job. The pay was unbelievable, it was an enormous step up from this small town. It would have been enough to get me my own place so I could divorce Carmen, which I was now intent on doing. I discussed this with her, and we could agree that when the job started in three months, she would not be going with me.

It was three months of bliss, me looking at apartments, buying some new boots. I started using some dating apps to try and meet women from the area, which I did. I met a nice young lady, her name was Melissa. Melissa knew about the divorce situation. We were discreet, we had seen each other about three times while waiting for my job to start. She and I were both eager at the new life that was in front of us.

One evening (I was back on night shift), I woke up around 5:00 pm and began to get dressed for my 6:00 pm shift. Putting on a police uniform takes a bit longer than just jeans and a t-shirt because of all of the equipment. I sat down and was tying my boots while Carmen was on the computer in front of me. She asked me about Melissa.

Carmen had gotten into my Facebook account somehow, and saw some messages between Melissa and me. I informed her that I had met Melissa and we had been talking. None of this should matter because we were getting divorced anyhow, and it would no longer be her business. She nodded, sad, but in agreement.

"Have you seen her?" She asked, still looking at the computer.

"Yes, we've met a few times." I'm still sitting and putting my boots on at this point.

"Have you slept with her?"

"Yes, I have." Perhaps I should have just lied, but I didn't care as much as I once had.

Now Carmen is standing over me, punching me repeatedly in the face while I block her strikes with my hand and am telling her to stop. In between me and the door is an enraged woman continuing to punch while I give warning after warning.

Enough is enough. I catch her next blow and slam her down on the couch next to me, one hand holding her still-closed fist, and the other on her throat—not squeezing or choking, but that was where my hand went when I grabbed her, and I wasn't going to move it until I knew she would stop.

I felt her finally relax, so I let her go. I stood up and left. I went to work, as I had done for years—gone to work no matter what we were going through at home.

As my shift started, I let my sergeant know what had happened. He had me write a report and told me to go about my shift. The thing was, this was my last day working here. The next day I would be gone and starting my new job hundreds of miles away from her. I just wanted to be done. I wrote the report and went on with my duties.

I get a phone call, from Melissa.

"I need you to talk to your wife," she says.

I hated that phrase 'your wife', I know we're still married, but come on.

"She's blasting me on social media."

"What?" I'm on speakerphone now, looking at Facebook. Sure enough, Carmen has tagged Melissa in posts on some public group and is using several derogatory terms to describe her.

The onslaught of comments from strangers is pouring in.

"I'm not sure what to do…" I tell Melissa on the phone.

"I'd like you to stand up for me. Say something."

So, I did. I commented on that post for the whole world to see. Something like "Carmen, after years of your drinking, cheating, and ditching out on the kids I have had enough. I told you that I am divorcing you, I'm done with you, and yes, I found somebody better."

My phone rings again. It's Carmen.

"What?" I said as I answered. I half-expected her to apologize or ask me to delete my comment. Something. What she actually said was so very shocking.

"I'm going to tell the cops you beat me up."

There it was plain as day, the most ludicrous thing she could have said. It was a lie, and if anything, SHE would be the one charged because SHE was the one who hit me.

"Then do it," I said, and hung up.

I referenced my partner earlier, cops don't drive around in pairs like you may see on TV (at least not where I've worked), but we worked the same shift and she was always the one to respond to the same calls as I. Her name was Christine.

Christine calls me.

"Hello?" I said, trying to sound work-ready as if nothing was going on as I had done for years.

"Look at the call screen, now!" She says and immediately hangs up.

There, on my computer, I see the incoming call from Carmen that I "punched and strangled her" before I left for work.

I stared at the screen for a moment, then returned to my supervisor's office to await the County Sheriff's Deputies who would soon be coming to question me.

Discussion

Domestic violence is about control. The abuser is a bully, trying to control you through means of force or intimidation. When that doesn't work, they may try other methods such as charm, guilt (threatening suicide), blackmail, or anything else. They want to control you. The scary fact is if they can't control you--the damage they may do is endless. Remember, they view you as property, and if they can't have you they will try to destroy you.

I don't really know if Carmen's intention was to cost me my job so that I would come back to her, the reality of actually losing me was too much for her to bear, or if she simply was being vengeful at this moment because she truly despised me.

But when you begin to force your way out of the box of control, an abusive person will find a way to shove you back in there--even if it means destroying your life, your career, your body, your reputation, your possessions, or anything else they can access.

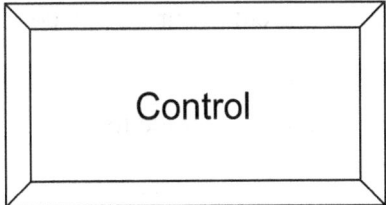

Freedom

Just outside the confines of the abuse and control, where you get your first breath of freedom, comes sabotage. The guardian that stands just out of view who will drag you back to your prison. Sabotage will tell you that you need the person, nobody else will love you or want you, you can't live on your own, the kids need you, or any other thing that is designed to break your concept of freedom and make you depend on that person again.

You are not somebody's property. They do not own you or your life, so it is not theirs to ruin… but they will if you give them that power and the delusion that they can get away with it.

They may cry and try to guilt you, they may threaten you, they may sabotage your life, but always remember - it is your life, not theirs.

Your spouse, partner, or kids should be your priority—there's nothing wrong with that. But all too often, we neglect ourselves and our own wellbeing for the sake of others and this is wrong. We cannot possibly be a good husband, wife, or parent if our own needs are not met.

What put me over the top and really made me decide to leave Carmen was a comment that someone mentioned to me, "children should see their parents smiling and sneaking a kiss, not being miserable". That comment was so true. What kind of father was I being by showing my kids "this is what a marriage is supposed to look like"… "drinking, fighting, lying, cheating, and hurting each other to get back at them."

I understood that I was wrong in my decisions to marry Carmen and "make it work", what the kids needed now was to see what love is supposed to look like. As a father, I owed them the service of teaching them what true love is… as this wasn't it.

Chapter 6
The Damage

When the deputies arrived at the station, they had already spoken to her and needed to hear my side. I gave them a copy of the report I wrote and recapped everything verbally—including my own infidelity.

Deputy #1 agrees that the best thing would be for me to get a hotel after work, and be out of town the next day—just to stay away from her.

Deputy #2, who was the Sergeant, believes he has enough cause to file charges. He cites me for domestic battery, has me remove my weapon and belt, and places me in handcuffs.

All the while, I can only think that this is ridiculous, and I am utterly appalled that it went to this extent. I was booked into jail, transferred to another facility (to avoid conflict of interest), and left alone in jail. I was placed in isolation, for my own protection, because of my law enforcement status.

After several days in jail, some colleagues bonded me out. I used the time to get an attorney, and to speak to my new Chief who was wondering why I hadn't shown up to work on my first day.

He informed me I no longer had a job. I pulled what was left from our joint account from an ATM, which was only a couple hundred dollars as Carmen had nearly emptied the account while I was in jail.

Carmen was a witness against me, which meant I couldn't contact her or go home. I couldn't see my kids, I couldn't even change my clothes.

I slept in my car once or twice, then got a hotel room before my court date so I could use the free razor/toothbrush/etc. to clean up before court.

At some point I called Melissa, she elaborated that she had

spoken to Carmen. Though I'm not sure what was discussed, Melissa made it clear that she was done with me.

This brings us to the point where I started this story. I had never felt so alone… ruined. Nobody in town would hire me now, I had nowhere to go and nobody to help me. The credit cards were maxed out, my bank account was empty, lawyer bills were stacking up, I missed my kids.

Despite now being unemployed, bills still came, my account quickly became overdrawn, and I saw no way out. I applied for every police officer job I could find, but the pending charges meant nobody would even give me a call.

Yet, I was so fortunate in my situation compared to many others. Many victims are beaten brutally or killed. The damage I suffered was more emotional and mental than physical.

I was eventually cleared of the charge in court. But I would find that the accusation alone would still prevent me from getting a job in law enforcement, even ten years later.

Part Two

Escape

Chapter 7
Be Committed

Getting out of a relationship is not always easy, especially when the relationship is riddled with abuse, manipulation, or addiction. If you have made a decision to leave a relationship, there are steps you can take to make the situation go as smoothly as possible.

The first step in the process of leaving a relationship is to commit. Being either 100% in the relationship, or 100% out of the relationship makes the process of transitioning less difficult. If you are indecisive, or keep breaking up then getting back together again, you are only making leaving the relationship more painful to you each time. If your significant other is manipulative or abusive, then being indecisive gives them more power and control over you.

Being in a relationship, but having one foot out of the door, is a sure way to ensure the relationship fails.

When I knew my marriage was over I was looking for a new life, a new job, a new girlfriend. It would have been much better to get divorced, and spend that time healing and recovering.

Commit entirely to your relationship, or commit entirely to bettering yourself for your next relationship.

Chapter 8
Assess the Risk

Once you have made the decision to leave a relationship, a risk assessment will help you determine what can go wrong, and how you can protect yourself.

Safety is always the priority. You need to ensure your safety (and your children if you have any). Do not hesitate to call 9-1-1 if you are in immediate danger.

If you are not in immediate danger, but threats have been made or you otherwise have concerns for your safety after you leave the relationship, speak to your local law enforcement agency about a protection order.

Find a trusted friend or family member you can stay with, or ensure that your significant other has somewhere that they can stay. Don't continue to stay in the same home with someone you have just ended a relationship with. Tensions will increase as you begin to separate your lives, and this situation can quickly become unsafe, or at least very uncomfortable.

If you feel you cannot safely leave the relationship, contact your local law enforcement agency, local domestic violence coalition, or the National Domestic Violence Hotline.

If you need to leave immediately, you can have law enforcement conduct a civil standby, a process where they come by so you can get your belongings from the house. You can leave immediately, then request a civil standby so you can get your things at a later time.

Space is something that you need to allow for healing. If you burn your hand on the stove, you absolutely must move your hand before it can begin to heal. Likewise, you must give yourself space from the person before healing can begin.

Do not attempt to stay friends after a break-up or divorce, at least not right away. Give yourself the space you need to heal. This may last days, weeks, months, years, or even forever—that is for you to decide, not them.

Cover-ups are things we use to mask damage. I mentioned earlier that I used women as a Band-Aid. We all know the benefits of using Band-Aids when we are hurt, but any parent also knows that a Band-Aid makes a child instantly feel better, even when it's not needed. Emotional Band-Aids make us feel better, even when they are not actually fostering any healing—they are just a cover-up.

Cover-ups can come in many forms, the biggest is jumping into another relationship right away. This does not allow you to heal, reflect, or grow from the previous relationship.

You may find that you want to work overtime now, sink into a depression, or get drunk. These things can all be cover-ups, they will temporarily cover your problem. When the cover-up is gone though, you will find that you have not healed at all.

Remember, it's okay to cry and it's okay to feel awful. But don't feel awful forever, slowly feel better as time goes on. In order to heal, you can't cover up the wound.

Manipulation is something that the other person may try in order to get you to stay in the relationship. This can come in many forms, it will usually reflect their conflict resolution skills at first, then they will try something more appealing to you.

For example, they may try to appeal to you with sex first—this is something that will keep you emotionally attached to them. Resist this effort, and they may become angry or accuse you of cheating or being not attracted to them.

Enticing you with sex, becoming angry, threatening, blaming or trying to make you feel guilty, using leverage such as children or money, threatening or attempting suicide, or using friends are all strategies of manipulation. Remember, once you have decided to leave, you are 100% committed to leaving and their efforts will not work. Do not be surprised by attempts to manipulate you.

Cleanly leaving the relationship is the best strategy. Leave immediately, do not have a lengthy conversation about leaving. Be respectful, but firm. Be honest, but to the point. Make sure that they are aware that the relationship is over, be clear, and physically leave.

Paperwork in some instances is appropriate. DO NOT neglect the appropriate paperwork because they make an agreement with you. If you are getting divorced, contact an attorney right away to protect your rights and interests. If there are children, contact an attorney right away. If you have mutual property or finances, contact an attorney right away.

A terrifying feeling is being blindsided by legal paperwork, being served with papers that you did not expect. Lawyers can be very expensive, but you need to protect your rights during this process.

If the relationship is just dating, and there are no legal concerns, be sure to pack all of your stuff before you leave so you don't have to ask for something back.

Don't be petty. Large amounts of money, property, and children are all worth fighting a legal battle over. Your sweater or other frivolous things are not worth fighting over. Being petty becomes an avenue for manipulation, "I want my deodorant back" just becomes a way that communication continues when it should have stopped, it becomes a way for them to see you when you need space to heal. They are hurting you.

If you did hire an attorney, get the essential things taken care of: child custody and visitation, large amounts of money, property (including vehicles), and debts.

You can buy more deodorant, you can replace the small things, but you can't heal when your hand is still on the stove that's burning you. You need space. If they are continuing to contact you and squabble over small things, they are keeping your hand on the stove.

Chapter 9
Be Proactive

Proactive steps will save you from a world of problems in the future. Looking back, there are so many steps I should have taken in my own divorce. Some I was too stubborn to take, while others I was not aware of.

Leaving early was something that I should have done. There was a point when I knew my marriage would not last, that should have been the point where I left. If I had left I could have contacted an attorney, and had time to heal and let the dust settle before attempting to find a new relationship.

Legal counsel was another step I wish I had taken sooner. I was afraid of the cost associated with an attorney, I also had hopes that we could "work things out ourselves".
If you are worried that you cannot afford an attorney, contact your local legal aid office. Legal aid can work with your financial needs. I felt so alone while my marriage was ending, and I was afraid of many things. Carmen threatened to take the children (along with many other threats she made). Legally speaking I had no right to stop her, at least not until a court order was in place.

Understanding manipulation would have helped me to realize that Carmen would try many things to get her way. Threats of taking the children, threats of suicide, and many others were employed against me. I had to accept that there are some things I simply can not control. I'm glad that Carmen did not end her life, but if she had, it would not have been my fault.

The court order granted us the right to alternate claiming the kids on taxes. When it was my turn to claim them, Carmen would ask for money. If I refused, she would threaten to move across the country with the kids. Eventually, I said "that's fine, I can't stop you, go ahead and move."

She didn't move. She stayed. I had to re-set my boundaries

with her.

Boundaries are very important when a relationship ends. If you have no children or legal issues to deal with, you may be fortunate enough to be able to cut all ties with the person. You may never have to speak to them again.

Having children means you must keep in contact with your ex, and that contact must be respectful. It does not mean that you need to take verbal abuse or manipulation, in fact, you have legal protection against those things. Divorce or custody decrees should (and typically do) include a section that guarantees your right to be treated with respect.

There were many phone calls with Carmen, that I should have hung up and asked her to text me instead. Every text could be printed and provided to the court if need be.

Setting boundaries and saying "no" will prevent further manipulation or abuse. Protect yourself, set boundaries early.

Part Three

Healing

Chapter 10
Aftermath

To briefly summarize the events that occurred after my arrest: I went to jail for a short period of time before some colleagues bonded me out. I hired an attorney, and the charges were dismissed relatively early in the process. But not before I lost my job, resisted suicide, spent what money I had, and maxed out my credit cards on hotel rooms and attorney fees.

I missed my children very much, because Carmen was a witness against me, I wasn't allowed to go home (where she was still staying). I couldn't call her to talk to the children either, there was nothing to do except wait.

The situation was a wreck. I was a wreck. Yet I still did not see my errors, I was very willing to blame Carmen for the things she had done and play the innocent victim. My martyrdom channeled into anger, I was furious at her for ruining my life.

It became so easy to point a finger at her for everything, including my wrongdoings; "I cheated on her, but only because of what she did".

For years, I went from job to job, trying to make enough to live on. I eventually had to move in with my parents when I started having to make child support payments after the divorce finally went through.

I dated a few people, but nothing lasted or worked out. After jumping from relationship to relationship, and going through breakup after breakup, I finally hit the wall.

After a particularly nasty breakup, I was finally broken to the point where I couldn't go on. At this point, I didn't understand a lot of what I was going through or the effects on my life...but I was going to learn.

Chapter 11
Wellness

I had grown up going to church when I was a child but had stopped as I got older. I always believed in God but found church to be boring. I considered myself to be a good person who believed in God and that should be enough, right?

Sitting in my room, depressed and broken, I decided I had to get out of this funk. I committed myself to a strict self-improvement regimen. It was simple: do something to improve physical, mental, and spiritual health every day for 30 minutes each.

30 minutes of exercise, 30 minutes of reading a book or watching something educational, and 30 minutes of Bible reading was easy to do as I sat in my room waiting for a job interview.

The trick with Bible reading is that you can't start at the beginning--start at John and move forward. The beginning of the Bible, the old testament, focuses on rules or law. The second half of the Bible, the new testament, focuses more on God's grace. Which was what I needed, a bit of grace and forgiveness, a bit of mercy.

As I read each day, I lowered my 30 minutes to just one chapter per day, and really tried to focus on what I read. I read through the writings of Paul and began to understand and embrace things that I had heard before but never truly understood.

During this time I learned so much, I couldn't possibly fit it into one single book. Instead, I'll share some of the principles that pertain to relationships.

Chapter 12
Giving up your Life

Here is the biggest statement I had to learn, say this over and over until you begin to truly grasp it: "I played a part in the successes and failures of the relationship."

Let me explain: there are two dangerous extremes of post-relationship resolution. The first is to put the other person on a pedestal, thinking that they are perfect and it's entirely your fault that the relationship failed. That way of thinking will depress you, it will cause you to feel inferior, lead to self-harm or addiction, and drop your self-esteem.

The other extreme is that you think you are perfect and it was entirely the other person's fault that the relationship failed. This is dangerous because it gives you an unrealistic expectation of relationships. You will expect your next partner to be perfect and begin to view any shortcoming as a deal-breaker. You will fail to take any responsibility for your faults. This is the extreme I was in after my marriage—I failed to see that I had done anything wrong.

Here is the middle-ground to these extremes: some things were not my fault, but I certainly wasn't perfect either. I want to learn and grow and do better next time.

A quick disclaimer: physical, mental, emotional, or sexual abuse is never your fault. These things are inexcusable actions from the other person and are not shortcomings that should be overlooked.

***

The two extremes I discussed above create two mentalities when there is conflict: "I won't change because I'm perfect. I need someone who loves me just the way I am, but they might need to change things about themselves." Or, "I'm flawed and must change whatever they need me to so that they will accept me." Again, both of these extremes are unhealthy.

What does the Bible say about this? Look at Ephesians 5:25,

"Husbands, love your wives, just as Christ loved the church and gave himself up for her."

I had heard this verse before and always took it to mean that I should be willing to die for my wife—it played to the image I had of husbands being protectors and providers. The reality is that you likely won't have to take a bullet for your spouse.

The word *life* in this context didn't mean my physical life, it was life in a different sense, the life I had chosen; my partying, my womanizing, my flirting, my sexual addiction. Often, the things that are 'normal' in the world, are not in line with what God intended for us. We may build a life based on what we think is normal, but it's seldom what's best. I should have been willing to give up my life for my marriage, instead of expecting my marriage to conform to my life.

This was an enormous turning point for me. I finally understood that all of my life I had been an "I won't change anything for anyone, and they must accept me the way I am" type of person. There were certain things I should have been willing to give up for my wife.

Now that I was divorced, there were things I needed to give up for my future wife. The most obvious was to treat my future wife like I care about more than just sex. From that moment on, I stopped sleeping with women and stopped dating all around. I remained single as I continued this journey of spiritual growth. I knew that the next woman I slept with would be my wife.

Discussion

"I'll change anything for my relationships" ———————————— "I'll never change for my relationships"

Where do you fit on the scale above? Are there things you are willing to work on for your future husband or wife?

Anything you are going to work on or change should be aligned with scripture. This isn't a trick or a secret, it's a simple principle: You must be the best husband or wife you can be BEFORE you get married. If you are already married, that's okay, it's not too late.

Make yourself into the man or woman that God created you to be. Then you can find the middle-ground of the scale. There are things you know you can work on, and things you know you shouldn't change or sacrifice.

***

Not sure of what things in your life can be sacrificed? Continue your Bible reading, your values should always align with scripture. Your spouse should never ask you to do something that disagrees with scripture.

All things should be done in love.

Chapter 13
What is Love?

What is love? What does it look like, feel like? Believe it or not, the Bible lays it out for us.

1 Corinthians 12:4-7 "Love is patient, love is kind. It does not envy, it does not boast, it is not proud. It does not dishonor others, it is not self-seeking, it is not easily angered, it keeps no record of wrongs. Love does not delight in evil but rejoices with the truth. It always protects, always trusts, always hopes, always perseveres."

These things may seem on the surface like simple terms, but it is difficult to follow these guidelines when we are upset, angry, or feel underappreciated.

If I think back to fights I had with my ex-wife, even though she was the one to become physically violent, I did not treat her in ways that were kind, I was seeking my own interests above hers, I brought up things she did wrong in the past.

Sound familiar? Of course, these things are how people fight. But this description of how we are meant to love is based on the way that God loves us. God doesn't bring up our sins, he doesn't get angry with us. Instead, he seeks to protect us. When we are sinning and in the wrong, God will love us all the same and help us work on the problem. That's what should be applied to your marriage: you and your spouse partner together to combat the problem.

When there is a mistake in a relationship, you can guarantee that your spouse is going to *fight with you* rather than *discuss it with you* if your actions put them on the defensive. If your actions are to insult and berate them, bring up the things they've done wrong, make them feel like a failure, or otherwise treat them harshly… why would they want to come to you with problems? Would you want to approach someone like that?

Here is the rule: your words should only build your spouse up, never tear them down. A relationship cannot function with one person causing harm to the other.

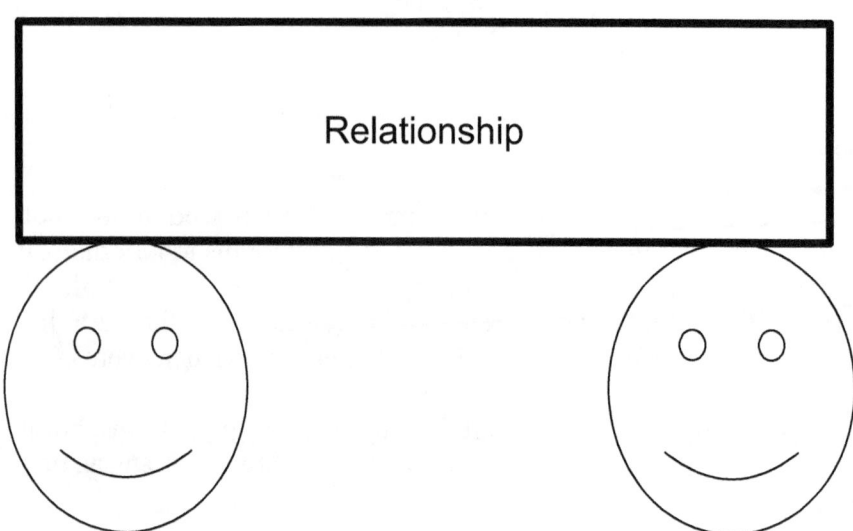

Look at the illustration above. Here we have a couple that is carrying a relationship. Here's the fact: A relationship weighs as much as two people can carry...no more, no less.

Of course, there are times that one is weak, struggling, or down and thus you have to carry a little extra weight temporarily. The problem comes when one person will not carry their weight, the other eventually is crushed beneath the heaviness of the relationship.

We fail to see when our actions are crushing our partner. Instead of encouraging, helping, and strengthening our partner, we are criticizing their effort, we are belittling them. As we criticize them, their motivation falls, and the weight becomes heavier on our end—making us feel frustrated and alone.

Ephesians 5:31 states "Therefore a man shall leave his father and mother and hold fast to his wife, and the two shall become one flesh".

Although the premise of this book is domestic violence, I share this point with good cause; the way you treat your spouse directly impacts the relationship and yourself.

If you insult your spouse, you not only verbally abuse them, but you are damaging your relationship and yourself at the same time. You are causing more weight to fall on yourself.

If you physically agress your spouse, you do so to your own self and future relationships. If you sexually abuse your spouse, you do the same to yourself, your relationship, and your future relationships.

Discussion

What are the images of love you have seen growing up in your own life? Are they in-line with the Bible's definition of love?

How can you adjust your image of love, how can you adjust the way you express your love to others—primarily, your spouse (current or future)?

I didn't just write this book for people that are already married or in a relationship, it applies to single people just as much. It is your responsibility to prepare yourself to be a healthy spouse. Otherwise, you enter into a relationship not being able to carry your full weight as we discussed in the illustration above.

We discussed giving up our lives for our spouse and what that meant, but what good will that be if we do not treat them the way they deserve?

Do we really expect God to be graceful and forgiving with our mistakes but we aren't willing to be as equally patient and gentle with our spouse? Your spouse is your partner for life. If you had a business partner, wouldn't you share your knowledge and experiences with them so that you could become a more efficient team? Wouldn't it be incredibly useful to make sure you had a peaceful workplace so that everyone was able to do their jobs?

Choose to build the house of your relationship on the foundations from the Bible, and the way that God teaches us to love.

How the world teaches us to love	How God teaches us to love
	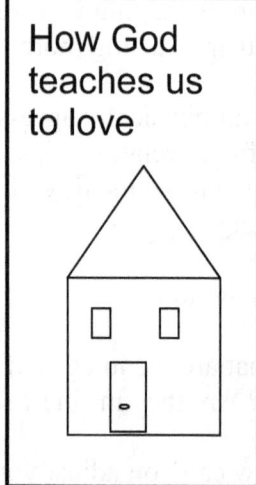

You need to build a house, you need to build your life. Before you pour the foundation, you need to choose which lot of land you are going to build on. Are you going to build on the land that is the way the world teaches to love, the way you may have seen growing up?

Even if you are not a Christian, the way the Bible teaches to love is an excellent guide—the perfect place to pour your foundation.

Instead of building on the way the world teaches to love, build the foundation of the relationship on the way the Bible teaches to love.

Let's think about ways we can be a partner and a teammate to our spouse; their biggest support, not their biggest critic.

Chapter 14
Codependency

Codependency is something I honestly didn't understand that I struggled with. It gripped me tightly and refused to let go, I was addicted. I was addicted to people, and I was addicted to sex with those people.

My commitment to celibacy had revealed just how deep I was stuck in that pit. I would come home from work, and instantly be on my phone looking to talk to someone, looking for attention from someone.

Even though I was no longer going out and looking for a hookup, I was still seeking that attention. Why? Because I wasn't secure with myself. In fact, I didn't even know who I was.

***

I will never forget the first time I heard a message from God. I always thought it was a bit of an exaggeration with people who said they "heard from God". This time, I did, as clear as day.

After my daily Bible study, I was praying and essentially asking God for a wife. I was ready to marry the right person.

God told me "prepare to live the rest of your life as a single man."

That crushed me, but only because I didn't understand what it truly meant. God wasn't saying that I would be single for the rest of my life. He was saying, I needed to be okay with being single the rest of my life.

This goes back to the concept of carrying a relationship. It would be unfair and devastating if I wasn't able to hold up my end. How could I offer her myself if I didn't even know who I was? I needed to learn how to be me; not the me that ran around drinking and chasing girls, but the me that I was meant to be!

I'm not sure how long this went on, but it was a relatively simple process: I continued the physical, mental, and spiritual exercises every day. I worked hard, I learned and grew, I surrounded myself with high-quality people who shared the same Christian views as me.

During this time I got asked out on more dates than ever before, I got offered no-strings-attached sex more than ever before in my life. All of which I refused, because I was hungry for something else now. I was tired of the temporary and ready for the forever!

One day, I was approached by someone I knew. It was strange the way it occurred, but let me set the scene:

Here is a gorgeous woman, strong, confident, she had worked hard her whole life and achieved great things, she was absolutely stunning. I was terrified. This wasn't someone that was damaged and looking for a guy to cling on to, she wasn't a hookup or a vulnerable girl. She was a queen, a woman that did not need me in her life. But for some reason I still don't quite understand, she wanted me in her life.

So we dated, then we became engaged, then we got married. All of this time we moved slower than I ever had before, we did everything right. We didn't jump into bed together, we didn't run around drinking or partying, we didn't move in together after a short time. She made me feel like I was the only man in her life, and I made sure to make her feel like the only woman in mine.

God's intervention in my life defeated the damage, the hurt, and the baggage of everything that occurred before. God will allow you to use his new foundation to build upon so that the past can be completely covered by his future.

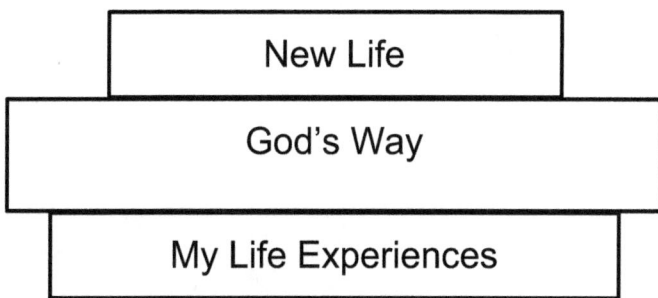

To this day I could not be more grateful that after so many years of stupidity, God was willing to help me stop, and start over the right way. And boy, was it worth it!

Daily Journal

The following pages are designed to help you focus on a particular topic each day and re-center your life onto a new foundation.

You will also receive important resources and information in this section.

Complete one journal entry each day for best results, but feel free to work at your own pace.

Day 1

Your safety must take highest priority. If you are being physically abused or are in immediate danger, please call 9-1-1.

If you are in a relationship that is physically abusive and unsure of who to contact, here are some resources for you:

The National Domestic Violence Hotline
https://www.thehotline.org/
(800) 799-SAFE (7233)

This organization offers free and confidential chat, consultations, and advice on next steps you can take.

See if your city or county has a domestic violence alliance or coalition, they can offer temporary support, sometimes including a place to stay while you get your affairs in order.

Journal

Am I in physical danger?

What am I most concerned about currently?

Who in my life can offer me support?

What changes or goals would I like to set for the next week?

Day 2

Self-identity is essential. You cannot be the best husband or wife you can be without understanding yourself.

Who does the Bible say you are?
- You are not a slave (Galatians 4:7)
- You are precious (Isaiah 43:4)
- You are strong (Philippians 4:13)
- You are forgiven (Psalm 103:12)

Think about who you know you are, who you want to be, and who the Bible says you are. How does this compare to who you have been told you are, or been led to believe you are because of other people's image of you?

Journal

Who have others told me I am?

Who do I want to be?

Who am I according to the Bible?

Day 3

Love is patient, love is kind. It does not envy, it does not boast, it is not proud. It does not dishonor others, it is not self-seeking, it is not easily angered, it keeps no record of wrongs. Love does not delight in evil but rejoices with the truth. It always protects, always trusts, always hopes, always perseveres. (1 Corinthians 13: 4-7)

Is this image of love what you have been shown in your life? How have your expectations been met or not?

If you need help or someone to talk to, please contact your local Christian church or local family counselor.

Journal

Has the love I've been shown in my life matched the Bible's description of love?

Has the love I've shown others matched the Bible's description of love?

Anything else I want to write about

Day 4

As you begin your own journey toward re-centering your life on a new foundation, create your own goals.

Your journey will differ from mine, you may find your own areas to improve upon that differ from the ones I have shared.

Use this day to check your progress on your own goals, create new goals, and just get your thoughts on paper. It is very helpful to document your growth on paper, but feel free to write about anything that you want today.

Journal

Day 5

Husbands should love your wives as Christ loved the church, so much that he gave his life for her (Ephesians 5:25).

What things in your life should you be willing to give up for a healthy marriage?

Do you struggle with addiction?

If you think you may need help with addiction, please contact:
American Addiction Centers
www.americanaddictioncenters.org
(866) 625-8712

What things in your life do you view as important, that you are not willing to give up for your spouse or future spouse?

Think of these questions in today's journal.

Journal

Day 6

Today you will step into a journey of growth free from the guides of this book. Use this page and the following pages to monitor your growth and progress. Remember, this is a never-ending journey.

At times you may feel down or helpless, please know you are not alone.

If you are looking for words of encouragement, please contact us at lovefireministries@gmail.com

If you or someone you know is having thoughts of suicide, please contact the National Suicide Prevention Lifeline at:
(800) 283-8255

Or visit www.suicidepreventionlifeline.org

Journal

Day 7

Verses I studied or topics I focused on today

Journal

Day 8

Verses I studied or topics I focused on today

Journal

Day 9

Verses I studied or topics I focused on today

Journal

Day 10

Verses I studied or topics I focused on today

Journal

About the Author

H.S. Daniels now lives with his wife and children in the beautiful mountains of God's Country. Together, they run their own business while also enjoying rewarding careers working with children.
Upon writing this book, Daniels began the LoveFire Project, an effort to share his experiences and the message of Jesus Christ with others. Daniels can be found sharing in schools and churches and can be contacted at lovefireministries@gmail.com

Other titles from Higher Ground Books & Media:

Wise Up to Rise Up by Rebecca Benston

For His Eyes Only by John Salmon, Ph.D.

Raven Transcending Fear by Terri Kozlowski

Redeeming Gethsemane by Daniel K. Held

The Bottom of This by Tramaine Hannah

Forgiven and Not Forgotten by Terra Kern

Out of Darkness by Stephen Bowman

Man Made by Grace by Willie Deeanjlo White

Healing in God's Power by Yvonne Green

Chronicles of a Spiritual Journey by Stephen Shepherd

The Real Prison Diaries by Judy Frisby

My Name is Sam…And Heaven is Still Shining Through by Joe Siccardi

Add these titles to your collection today!

http://www.highergroundbooksandmedia.com

Do you have a story to tell?

Higher Ground Books & Media is an independent Christian-based publisher specializing in stories of triumph! Our purpose is to empower, inspire, and educate through the sharing of personal experiences.

Please visit our website for our submission guidelines.

http://www.highergroundbooksandmedia.com

www.ingramcontent.com/pod-product-compliance
Lightning Source LLC
Chambersburg PA
CBHW061501040426
42450CB00008B/1444